THANK YOU FOR STAYING
By: Melody Dalili

Thank You For Staying © Melody Dalili
Arrangement and edition © The 5th Woman, LLC.
All rights reserved.
This book, or parts thereof, may not be reproduced in any form or by any means electronic, digital, or mechanical, including photocopy, scanning, recording, or any information storage and retrieval system, without written permission from the publisher except in the case of brief quotations embodied in critical articles or reviews.
For information, contact The 5th Woman Books.

The 5th Woman, LLC, Publisher
www.the5thwoman.com

Cover art by: Leah Dalili
Author photo: Margaret Smith
Design & Production: Rhea Carmon

ISBN: 979-8-9881547-2-3

THANK YOU FOR STAYING

POEMS

MELODY DALILI

INAUGURAL YOUTH POET LAUREATE OF KNOXVILLE, TENNESSEE

THANK YOU FOR STAYING

In August of my junior year of high school, I performed my first spoken word after 7 years of hiding my love for poetry. As much as I want to make it sound as professional and classy as possible, the first thing I said at the mic was "I can't feel my hands!"

That one moment folded into a whole new relationship with words-- saying them out loud. Being able to use my voice on a stage and project it to the world was the biggest contribution to the most revolutionary chapter of my life. I cried. I complained. I yelled. I laughed. I was scared. I experienced lighthearted summers and bitter winters of emotions all behind the microphone, but most importantly, I loved it all. I couldn't feel my hands, but I could feel the power behind each syllable that rolled off of my tongue. I would have never expected those special moments to transform into becoming the first ever Youth Poet Laureate of Knoxville.

Being in this new position has evidently taught me so much, but even amidst all of the new changes, I think the most crucial part of the journey was remembering what brought me here. I am so in debt to my father, who has so beautifully played both parental roles and is the definition of childlike joy. Leah, my younger sister and illustrator of this book cover, who has listened to my spoken words and revisions dozens of times in preparation for the stage and would do it again and again in a heartbeat. She is my best friend and absolute twin flame, my rock and usually my voice of logic. In the most genuine way possible, I am forever thankful for the friends who have shared their days with me: Abigail Russell, who has brought me closer to myself and my Creator, a walking embodiment of Grace and unconditional love, the most gentle soul I know who has shepherded me into adoring hugs again; the Lord, who found me in the middle of writing this book and sweetly shifted the way I saw the world; Ms. Toth, my Advanced Creative Writing teacher, who was one of the first people to believe in me; and Annalise Bishop, who wrote me a heartfelt letter about our friendship a few months before I was titled Knoxville's Youth Poet Laureate. She gave it to me out of the blue and when I asked her why she wrote it, she told me she felt that she "just had to." That letter was full of words I still hold close to me, but the final line stood out to me the most: "Thank you for staying."

After years of trying to make sense of unresolved childhood trauma and sinking into the numbest downfalls of my depression and cPTSD, those words were exactly what I needed.

Annalise passed it on to me, and now I'm passing it on to you.

Thank you for staying. I don't know how much you need to hear that, but that simple appreciation has saved my life. It is so easy to discredit yourself for just being here, but the fact that you are alive is extraordinary. I encourage you to take this message and pass it on to your Annalise, your Abigail, your Ms. Toth, your family by blood and by choice. I thank you for being here, and I thank them too.

THANK YOU FOR STAYING

has no one told you yet?

i saw you in my dream last night
you were awake and
alive and
your lips weren't quite blue yet and
your hands were still warm

i touched your face and told you
you were dead—
breaking the news to you the same way
it was broken to me—
and you smiled and said
no, i'm not

now it's 2 AM,
24 hours past,
and i stay up
trying to figure out the difference between
a dream and a nightmare,
between reuniting and discovering.
i stay up and wait for an answer like
a skinny dog at your door

Thank you for staying

and i am tired.
but i am afraid of falling asleep
because
i can't look you
in the
eye

am i the only one who knows?
has no one told you yet?

Thank you for staying

the robins are not singing this morning

the robins are not singing
this morning

i peek through closed blinds
just to watch
autumn unfold outside of my window
and i hate the songbirds
for their absence
because
i can still hear my mother weeping
in the bathroom

the frigid air
is pressed up against my window
like desperate ocean waves
sprawling up against the shore
again
and again
and again
my hands are afraid of the glass--
frosted over and
painful to touch--
the ache that comes with loving Mother Nature
is similar to the ache that is tied with loving my mother

i am a liar at five,
a criminal in kindergarten
and
a burden
in my own home

---

thank you for staying

the thermostat is on 67 and not 66
i am wrapped in two blankets and not one

but
still,
the air is warm and
i am thankful
for not having to spend the evening
on the other side of the window
in a bitter autumn
for not being a hungry, shivering dog
chained to the side of a barn
wagging his skinny tail at a whistle
but pulling-- wobbling-- away at a reach;
for not being a robin
unfolding her wing to wrap it around her hatchlings,
trembling and too tired to sing;
for not being a mighty, emerald oak tree
painted over with a dull brown and
robbed of his leaves;

the air is still warm
and i am still thankful
but
my mother is still weeping
behind a closed door

i want to show her how warm our living room is
she is so busy
whimpering
like the animals
locked outside,

THANK YOU FOR STAYING

i fear she is missing it

so
i grin and dance over to the bathroom door
and reach up
to turn the handle
pushing it open with both arms,
glancing at the counter first

there are
containers and jars tipped over and
perfume bottles
broken and
spilling into the sink

i look at my mother in the mirror
and she looks at
a piece of herself
and my heart is gutted.

my mother is cutting her hair.
she lifts strands and haphazardly
hacks
them off with
the same safety scissors i
learned how to use
the school day before

the air is frigid again.
she sobs and discards the pieces she doesn't like
and i am surprised the scissors aren't
pointed at me.

Thank you for staying

i watch her dark brown hair fall like autumn leaves
onto the marble tile
and i hate the songbirds
and i hate my mother
for bringing
the bitter season outside my window
into the warmth of my very own home.

thank you for staying

another tomorrow

i still feel like
you are coming home
soon

Thank you for staying

my body is a home, can i throw away the key?

these eyes--
slightly tainted yet still unfazed--
are the open windows,
and the ones who let me see truth

these arms, these hands--

graffitied in scars--
are the dusty, untouched doors inside
may these hands not flinch or pull away
when held for the first time,
but may they not be forced open

these shoulders--

a little shaky when it storms--
are the walls that hold me together
and are the ones who keep me guarded

i have tried to rent her out before

hoping someone else would
manage the squeaky floors
i have tried to pack my things
and stay somewhere else for a few nights
thinking that abandoning her
will make everyone forget that she belongs to me

this lost body

is the home where i will endure
the floods, hurricanes, and tornadoes
the home where i will host the most chaotic parties
the home where i will survive
the nights with no electricity
calling her my home
leaves a dryness in my throat,
a ringing in my ears,

Thank you for Staying

and an aching
within the corridors of my head
but believe me,
i have tried to mold this body
into all but what she is
just to figure out her concrete walls
don't like to break

so i will polish the somber floors,

dust off the debris within the corners,
and water the weeping plants
until the aching finally leaves my head
until the rooms finally learn to open the curtains
until the corridors finally learn how to sit in silence

and when that time comes--

when the aching is finally emphasized as unwelcome--
we just might be able to
hear ourselves speak

Thank you for staying.

are you sure you want to leave so early?

my head aches so violently
i can track my pulse without trying
with each thump i hear, i wince
forced to remember that it hasn't left me yet

it's incredible

beautiful even
how my body can nudge me
and let me know that her lights are still on
my heart is still beating
my leg is still bouncing
my eyes are still full of water
is it a miracle or a curse?

a thankful doctor and a weeping newborn--

maybe each migraine
each heartache
each tremble
is a blessing

a reminder that i am still

alive

✷thank you for staying ✷

my 5 AM pottery class

last night i signed up for a pottery class
on impulse before i went to sleep
i have dreams of artists giving lectures--
trying to convince me
that my hands are worthy
of sculpting something incredible

a trinket here or there,

my home could use a pot or two
especially if made by the soul living in it;
adding accents to the furniture i barely use
but purchased for the rare chance of company

my shelves are empty

my nightstand is bare
my kitchen counter has tumbleweeds
rolling across its dusty granite
i am so excited to put something there to fill the open space
and on the day that someone stays over
we will talk all about it
the air will never get cold with silence--
a disease my body has yet to get used to

so the day of the lesson,

i left my house an hour early
saving wiggle room for traffic by surprise
on a groggy wednesday morning

but when i arrived to the appointment--

hair pulled back, apron fastened,
arms wide open--

Thank you for staying!

i found myself being molded

twisted and turned into

cats and dogs
peeled and polished
into kitchenware
modeled for someone else's kitchen

counters
but mine are still deserted

in all the glossy, expensive porcelain

displayed around me
i catch my reflection and can't help but stare
why do i look like that?

you are art

they whisper
but i am not shaped as i had imagined
a vase with a body too skinny
a smooth, polished teapot
but i praise all of my fractures
you are art you are art you are art
they will want to see you this way
but i shake my head
over and over again
i thought i signed up to be the sculptor

the hands that longed to express themselves

through something greater than poetry
now caught picking and pulling
pushing and molding
trying to reshape
a body no longer mine

the kiln, the artist, some porcelain, and me

but what have i truly become?

Thank you for staying! xoxo

i still see you in the flowers behind my house

you still look the same
exactly how i had remembered
identical to what i dreamt of us--
wishfully running through a tulip field
though   probably   standing   shoulder   to
shoulder like strangers in a busy subway

but now it's just us two
in an overflowing room
loud with sounds of mourning
my eyes occupied
my heart thumping
my hands a little shaky

do you still remember me?
do your atlantic eyes still remember
the dark chocolates in mine?

i guess it's just us two
you and me
me and you
hiding under a blanket of stars
i just wish we could go back
to whatever it was before
though my body still trembles like it did
when i first stood before you

Thank you for staying

wake up - i beg
wake up wake up wake up
come back
i am still waiting for you
there are more sunsets to see

do you hear me pleading?
making offers with mistresses in the afterlife
i give them my heart and they will give you a few more seconds with me
will your eyes flutter open and catch mine again
or will they rest forever?

i grab your yellowish hands
and lean into the wooden box
maybe if i yell loud enough
my voice will do the impossible
and travel through incredible boundaries
just to get a last word in

i love you
i love you i love you i love you forever

i love you for your sunshine
your golden hair, your glowing smile
from ear to ear and wrapped around the earth
i love you for your sunshine
a hug from behind in the midst of silence
a dance in the pouring rain
i love you for your sunshine
and i can remember all of these things i ache for
just by glancing at you once again

Thank you for Staying

a dim, lifeless shell
but you are sunshine somewhere else

i love you like the stars love the moonlight
i miss you like the stars miss the moonlight

but i hate you ten times over
for choosing an open casket

Thank you for staying !

quality time

my grandfather and i sit around our dining table
for a tea party in our empty house
i spent twenty minutes before this
rummaging in the cabinet,
choosing two perfect cups
for us to drink out of

and although i am barely old enough
to qualify for kindergarten
i insist on hosting our great gathering
offering to pour him some grape caprisun
out of a teapot three times the size of my palms,
but he shakes his head and says
his cup is already full

so i pull out yellow construction paper
and dull colored pencils
in the hello kitty purse
i brought from my room upstairs
and i curl my lip
as i try my hardest to doodle a kitten

i show him my artwork once i'm done
and in his broken english he tries
to tell me how nice it looks

cat, look so soft
you draw?
and i fix my posture
and nod my head
and turn the paper over

Thank you for staying!

and slide it to him
and i tap my pointer finger on the table.
your turn, i whisper.

he spends some time
moving the pencil with white knuckles
as my legs kick back and forth
in waiting

while he proudly hands the paper back to me
i look over his illustration
my heart swears he is an artist but
his work is not what i thought it would be

an animal with ears too big for its head
it has five legs and two tails and
a neck too long and
a nose too short and
three eyes all looking at me

i giggle at his imperfect masterpiece
and he lets out a chuckle too

with both of our pinkies up,
i carefully sip on my juice box
and he finishes his sixth bottle of beer

---

thank you for staying

astronomy

when i was twelve i learned that
stars
are made up of gas and
undergo enough pressure to
squeeze
atoms of light together,
so maybe
if i had hugged you
tighter or
more often
we could have become
something
worth looking at

thank you for staying

nature vs nurture

growing up i admit i
resented my father for
his inattentiveness

for looking away when
i reach the climax of my thrilling story and
begging me to repeat it all again,
for asking what my friends' names are
after they introduce themselves,
for not knowing the answer to my math problem
when tears are rolling down my face at the dining table

i was raised watching my parents' friends--
so close i call them *aunt* and *uncle*--
scold him
for not listening
and i, too, began to correlate
confusion with
carelessness

now i'm 17 and
sitting alone on the tile floor of my
high school hallway
after asking to be excused from all the
noisy distractions of a silent classroom to
finish reading tangled words on a page;
my eyes look over it once
and twice
and three times
and four and

Thank you for staying

tears well up in my eyes and
my hands are in clenched fists and
the inside of my cheek is bitten and bleeding
and the still, quiet air is so deafening

in all of my retries and
rereads,
my stinging lips just want to mutter
the words i have been conditioned to loathe:
"i do not
understand."

Thank you for staying

thief

sometimes i think you were so
used to taking and
taking and
taking you
forgot to look at what your white knuckles were hoarding
because
you took my fear with you as well

Thank you for staying.

growing pains

i am afraid of the aches that come with aging,
the stumbles that partner with prospering, and
the days when i will look into the mirror and see
you looking back at me.
i try to imagine what it would be like to
stare death in the face but i've
already done it before i even opened my eyes,
my first steps taken on an ocean of love i still
am trying to baptize myself in

call it a growing pain or

label it as a chronic illness,
either way, i will always be
wondering how my body can
forgive
when it refuses to
forget

Thank you for Staying!

i will love you even if _____

i love you, i say
like there is scripture in every syllable

and
i will love you even when there is a
bottle of vodka pressed up against your chapped lips and
i will love you when your shaky hands signal for another
and i will love you when you call me and i have to
decipher whose voice it is and
i will love you when you wake up and forget about it all
and i will love you when you read this and
have to question who it was written for

the bottle you cling onto and
the smoke underneath your tongue and
the slurring of your speech
do not weep when they see you crumble into a
shell of who i fell in love with
friendship is too valuable to
come with a price
but i loved you and
i love you and
i will love you until you are
whole again and i will still love you after that

i would unlock my rib cage and
give my heart to you
if you asked for it
and maybe then i might recognize all of you again

Thank you for staying

"say you're sorry"

the train by my house wakes me up every night
it interrupts my treasured slumber but
the earth keeps turning

the lightning invites itself to every storm and
craves to be the center of attention
i watch Mother nature at war from my window but
still, the earth keeps turning

the graveyards nurture what i can no longer tend to
the heavens cradle and hold what were robbed of me and
even when i ask for it to stop,
the earth will still keep turning

the train and the lightning and the graveyards
do not say they are sorry
the Creator
does not owe me an apology for taking up space

sometimes i catch myself walking like i'm
trying not to make the ground uncomfortable by my footsteps
but one day,
i swear i will be free of debt, too

Thank you for Staying!

life would be easier

if i could find a way to
love you less

thank you for staying

maybe, or possibly, or probably not

for all of my life, i have
abided in every gray area

i have chosen to love with
one foot in and one foot out of the door,
i have used the word *maybe* like a
morning mantra,
my head does not know how to nod or shake in a
yes or no

so I end up making a home
where no one else wants to settle
and try to call it my own,
like a spider weaving a village in the
forgotten corners of someone else's world.
acknowledgement is a synonym for destruction—
when i am seen, i start to pack my bags
in preparation for
the next migration
i have tried to pacify the pressure of polarization
by choosing to not decide at all.

but now i am starting to feel the
discomfort in isolation;
i am both too much and not enough, and i
become the gray spaces i hide in when i
refuse to pick a side.

Thank you for staying

i hear *i love you*
and my mouth hesitates to commit
to a smile or a frown
so it cowers in a straight line.

Thank you for staying

the search

i have wandered everywhere

all the way to the end of the river where
you said you would meet me
up the weathered oak tree that was
just a sapling when
you told me you loved me
past the places we raced toward
to catch every pink and purple and orange
in the sky
under the waterfall that bellows the same way
you did when you stuck your head out of the sunroof
down that backroad we loved

i have peered up into the heavens and
dared to scan the underground,
folded my heart inside out and
examined every crater,
untwisted and retwisted and flipped the
kaleidoscope behind my eyes
just to realize
you are never coming back

Thank you for staying

my love language

i have spent my days observing
how the day loves the night
how the sun loves the moon
how red loves purple across the entire rainbow
how each star in a constellation loves another
how the flowers love their roots and
how my frigid fingertips can love a campfire

and i realized i can love you
the way i have watched the world love herself:
from a distance

thank you for staying

where i'm from

i am so close to myself yet
so far from where i come from

THANK YOU FOR STAYING

anatomy sermon

your eyes tear up and squeeze shut and
diverge away from others
your hands shake and bleed and
close into a fist
your arms wrap around a stranger who
melts and dissolves into your chest
your stomach cries in the feeling of abandonment
and your heart whispers for attention
your vital organs are tugging on your sleeve and
begging for you to stay alive

they will die trying to
convince you that
you are worthy

will you believe them?

Thank you for staying

i thought i saw you today. did you know that?

i have a fading memory of
when you shared some time with me.
your hourglass, low on sand but
i guess you were the only one who knew it

your shoes were tied so tight it
bothers me to even say
any part of you could be
contained and
held together so neatly

in that memory you had not died yet
the flowers did not weep every october
the earth did not stop to reroute its orbit and
consider going back for you
i did not have to correct someone
when they talked about you in the present tense

now,
my shoes are untied and
i hear your eulogy in every belly laugh
i find your tombstone in the
sunset and in the
bricks of your house and in the
rice cakes on aisle 9.
i used to think that meant that
my world molded into a graveyard

---

thank you for staying

but i think it means your memory is so
rich and saturated, it has
become the sweetest friend of mine.
it perches like a raven on my
shoulder. its wings are not clipped but
still, it stays.

Thank you for staying

my native language

being raised in an asian household, i can
remember how well i
used to speak mandarin

a language so complex yet so pure, i
admit i am still
startled when i hear it again.
i confess to envying the elegance in every
syllable
and i have a hidden heartache for
where i come from—
a puppeteer, pulling
on my heart strings
in every word

although i am not as fluent as the
rest of my own,
their sayings will
always feel like home.
"ai yah!"
for when you are startled;
"nǐhǎo ma?"
for when you want to check on
someone you love;
"xièxiè!"
for when you are feeling thankful;

"wǒ ài nǐ."
means
i love you—
did you know that?

Thank you for Staying

i didn't either.
i've spent a lifetime trying to
belong
in my own culture,
trailblaze
in my own tradition,
blend into
my own ancestry
yet i had never heard it once

Thank you for staying.

my brain is a battleground

my brain is a battleground,
villages saturated with fire and
the taste of metal in the frontal lobe

sometimes i want to
hold a grudge
against it
for the parts of its job
that i disapprove of.
each suture is a fault line,
each groove is the daybreak of an
earthquake waiting to crumble and
fold into itself like
the shell i am less afraid to be.
i resent it for
forgetting
what i wanted to cling onto and
remembering
what pours resin into my throat
but it is working overtime just to
give me the capacity to complain

✶ thank you for staying ✶

there are
pieces of me in what is
trying to kill me,
and there are
pieces of me in
what is trying to keep me alive.
it is a civil war—
both sides do not know what they are
fighting for
but their bellies tumble over the
bite of
losing.

how will you look at the tide?

when i was seven, my father warned me
that the ocean currents
could drag me under

to sweep me up from underneath like a
weighted blanket and
hold me there,
my body kicking away in fear of
its love language

and every vacation since, i confess there
will always be a part of me
that ruins the mood with a
what if—
i look out into the sea and imagine i am
dragged across the
sharpened fingernails of coral,
drowned in the heart of something beautiful

i wonder how many oceans
we miss out on
because we are too afraid to die.
i wonder how many more chances
we would have taken if
we knew we would have made it out alive

Thank you for staying! xoxo

surrendering to the safety of the shore,
taking ten steps backward
and calling it growth,
putting on the floaties with an empty
excuse, bending the definition of courage to
convince ourselves that we are brave.

we walk along the shoreline like we
dare to balance on a tightrope between
life or
death,
but the two true outcomes are
living or
surviving

Thank you for staying

sticks and stones may break my bones, and words will hurt me too

my body is covered in wilting bandaids,
peeling off like
weeping flowers to
reveal the fruit of violence

with fists shaking in anger,
we lunge at our own walls, leaving
one dent for every tragedy we
have lived through and
one more for every *"I cannot believe
this could have ever happened,"* and
one more for every *"i never saw it coming"*

and
one more for every person
who wants to believe that violence
is the antidote to a plague that is
prescribed alongside our first breath,
a blood-stained piece of floss that we
weave in between our teeth to
prevent the hollow cavity that grows
at the same rate as the
empty nausea in my stomach

our knuckles
rebound and shatter
and we lift our aching hands
up to our ears
like a conch shell,

Thank you for Staying

listening with desperation to
the ocean of blood
lunging back at us
and each time
the tide crashes and recedes, it repeats the same message:

wake
up

Thank you for staying !

you are half of me, but i am all of you

in between the hurried shovels
of steaming rice onto her
tongue, my mother tells me
the dangers of
eating too much:

you will get fat, and
no one will want to be seen with you
as i spoon another bite into my mouth

she is puzzled at my ignorance
my stomach is a thief who is
too confident in its presence,
made itself too welcome in its high chair

i feel the groans and rumbles of hunger and
i realize we are quite the same.
i know
it did not ask to be here but
now it will pay the burden
for existing

i take another bite, the rice cold with
the curse of waiting, but
i still do not regret
gambling with my mother

sickening,
she bids, her fists rolled—
do not know when to stop and

Thank you for staying!

do not know your place,
think you can take what you want but
you are nothing

it is a two player game of mahjong:
we are competing for the
comfort inside our own
home, and
my life is being wagered
in the center of our dining table.
i fire back at her with
another bite of rice.

you are just like your father,
she shoots, a final attempt at winning it all.

but with that
and that alone,
i am crowned victor

Thank you for staying

a promise that was kept

everything is going to change.

from summer to fall to winter to spring,
the limelight will shift and
give its glory to each and
every season but
i promise you have never seen this one before.

familiarity
will place a rock in your throat and
you find a way to make a home
in the wildfire.
i promise
if you water your wounds
you will be busy
observing the wildflowers
blooming from underneath your skin

folding inside out and upside down,
the world will be
nothing like you expected it to be and
i promise
it will be something
beautiful

thank you for staying

the butterfly and hermit crab

she carefully pours me cranberry juice
into a wine glass.

her mother is sitting on the porch, legs
propped up on the dusty ottoman,
fingers cradling her own glass of
alcohol.
i wonder if she has ever
hugged her daughter the same way she
holds the bottle up to her chest,
or if she has ever
gently kissed her child
the same way her
lips rest on the rim of the glass

we are children— teenagers,
craving to be adults—
too big for our own bottles but
too young for a bottle like her mother's.
i watch her mother return inside just for
her fourth refill, and i
wonder if the butterfly has ever
felt homesick for her cocoon, or
if the hermit crab has ever
considered abandoning the
crushing weight of her own home.

i want friends to feel like family, but
a family that is not mine.

Thank you for staying

what it means to be a woman

the first time
i put on a dress,
i traced the cold zipper
up the raised trail of my spine

and i think the dress was as shaken as i was--
holding up a broad pair of shoulders,
confused which parts to cinch and
which parts to hide,
the strongest muscles, a parasite in all of
the wrong places.
to raise my voice is to jeopardize my
noble seat in delicacy

but
the dress and i can both agree we
were never meant to coexist--
and in its eyes alone, my
boldness to identify as a woman is
a fraud woven in itself:
a wolf in sheep's clothing,
pulling up the v-neck that sits
too low on my chest,
clawing at the fleece that
hugs every curve too tight,
biting off the fragile features of femininity
with jagged teeth

weeping over wool,
wilting over womanhood

Thank you for staying

the seventh day

it is sunday
and i am standing
shoulder to shoulder in a crowd
saturated in unfamiliar,
and i thank the knot in my stomach for
deciding to stay home

i huddle close to the
girl i walked in with
and watch the couple in front of us
unlock hands
just so they can
lift them up towards the light
in worship

my friend has her eyes closed,
chin lifted,
palms open,
lips moving quietly,
and i hope the One she is praying to can hear how
thankful she is,
and i hope He knows i still haven't counted
how many exit doors are in here,
and i hope He knows my open palms do not want to cover
my ears anymore,
and i hope He knows i made it out,
and i hope He knows i made it in,

Thank you for staying.

and i hope He sees the possum in me
belly up, breathing deeply,
and i hope He knows it isn't playing dead but
just learning what it means to rest.

to be fostered

as a child of something greater is to
feel the spinning coin in my stomach
finally land on its back
it is not the break of thunder or the
rattling of hollow bones, but
the stillness in looking up and believing.

the grateful possum lying on its spine with
its rib cage sprung open like a bear trap,

the two children in the church
rocking back and forth with
the veins in our belly-up forearms lifted
towards the sky.

don't ask me what the definition of home is just yet,
but i think i'm onto something

Thank you for Staying!

the instinct to care

barbed wires dance around
a square of tended grass and
the horses have made smooth trails from
failing to reroute, start something new

i would hate to be raised that way

to think i'm discovering it all
when there's a chain tugging my ankle
it burns circles in my skin
and i think it's hugging me back

somewhere

there's a mother bird
leaving a nest of needy, weeping hatchlings
tired and
hungry,
she finds a box of nails and
believes she unearthed a feast

a doe lets a young wolf

sleep in the bedding
and her fawn is killed when she wakes

an old hound picks up a

little, abandoned squirrel and
places it among her own pups
she curls around its body all night but
it still loses its breath in the morning

Thank you for staying

i run in burning circles of
whether you tried hard enough
if you were sick or just didn't care
if you knew what you did or
were just doing what you were taught

either way it's hopeless
the bird, the doe, the hound
confused and left empty
their children held too tight it killed them
you couldn't have loved me in a way that mattered

Thank you for Staying!

the sting of independence

too many times
i insist on indulging in the glory
of being alone--

the absence of footsteps in the
dead of night,
a table set for one at dusk

how can you rest in your empty house,
bundled in the quiet?
a housecat blinded by the limelight,
blinking, blanking,
ears pinning themselves back,
the audience chanting too loud:

sleep, sleep, sleep, sleep

only the nothing holds too much
it is heavy on my shoulders when i
open my front door to silence

when my eyes flutter shut
my father is telling me about the miraculous
soup he made out of accidents,
and my sister is leaping out of the
passenger seat after i promise to
buy her a book under five dollars,
and i am not afraid, but humbly reminded
of what a privilege it is to
be
alive

thank you for staying

and to dust i will return

winter arrives and the
dandelions on my porch begin to wilt and hunch over,
and i feel like i just planted them yesterday

they remind me of the eerie fact that i, too, will one day
die

i do not hold the godly power to know
when i will go

who i will see again

or where i will go to

all i can do
is pray my atoms be
recycled,
be transformed,
be not created nor destroyed,
and
i might just be lucky enough to be
somewhere in a baby's first smile,
or
harbored in the glowing belly of a firefly,
or
still, silent, in a waterhole
both lions and gazelles slip a sigh of relief to see

Thank you for staying

to die is not to leave;
it would be the greatest honor to come back in
the dandelions you blew out on your front
porch, your mother yelling, screaming the
weeds, the parasites
we just dug them out yesterday,
as they rock back and forth with the wind

it's a shame,
you thought,
that something this yellow would be seen as as a
burden

Thank you for staying!

Thank You For Staying Signatures

ella castelloe
abigail russell
kaela mciver
melody dalili
tyrone beach
teleia burns
allison comer
corey hodge
katherine cormack
dayton kennedy
mikaela brock
angie mccarter
kara doyle
john bartlett
stephanie evans
andi tenry
clare brimer
natalie mcmichael
annalise bishop
margaret huffstetler
elizabeth plewniak
shannon smith
leah dalili
valarie cagle
sarah archer
chloe pool
maggie smith
cara vaughn

Made in United States
Orlando, FL
31 July 2023